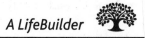

A LifeBuilder

2 CORINTHIANS
Finding Strength in Weakness

*11 studies
for individuals or groups*

Paul Stevens

With Notes for Leaders

Scripture Union is an international Christian charity working with churches in more than 130 countries.

Thank you for purchasing this book. Any profits from this book support SU in England and Wales to bring the good news of Jesus Christ to children, young people and families and to enable them to meet God through the Bible and prayer.

Find out more about our work and how you can get involved at:

www.scriptureunion.org.uk (England and Wales)
www.suscotland.org.uk (Scotland)
www.suni.co.uk (Northern Ireland)
www.scriptureunion.org (USA)
www.su.org.au (Australia)

ISBN 978 1 78506 277 3

First published in the United States by InterVarsity Press 1990, revised 2001.
© Paul Stevens

First published in the United Kingdom © Scripture Union 2004, reprinted 2005, 2009; this edition 2015.

British Library Cataloguing-in-Publication data: a catalogue record for this book is available from the British Library.

Printed in India by Thomson Press India Ltd

Image credit: vernonwiley/iStock by Getty Images

Contents

Getting the Most Out of 2 *Corinthians*

Life is relational. We hope and hurt the most about relationships with people who matter to us: A special friend we are in danger of losing. An employer who misunderstands our actions. A spouse who is distant and cold. A brother in Christ who has spoken behind our back. A family member long estranged. These may be parts of the web of relationships that make up our lives. When a valued relationship is hanging by a slender thread, we are often at a loss to know what to say or do. Should we tell the truth even if it hurts? Should we avoid confrontation? Should we share what is going on inside us even if it shows we are weak and struggling, far weaker than we would like others to know?

Second Corinthians is all about relationships—not perfect ones but real ones. In this letter the apostle Paul reveals that he is struggling deeply in his relationship with the believers in Corinth. Though he founded this church, they have apparently rejected him. This letter is an attempt at reconciliation. What made Paul's relationship more complicated was the seeming contest between Paul and his converts. The Corinthians were enjoying charismatic ecstasy. They had their orators, theologians, super-saints and super-apostles. They were strong, wise and triumphant. Paul, in contrast, was weak, foolish and seemingly a failure.

In similar circumstances most people try to use strength and wisdom to win their way back. They create just the right leadership image. But Paul chose to pour out his soul to them, trusting that in the process Christ would be revealed. In this letter Paul is both medium and message. This great Christian leader takes the enormous risk of telling how confused, upset and weak he is. In 1 Corinthians Paul lets us see inside a first-century church. But in 2 Corinthians Paul lets us see inside a first-century Christian, the apostle himself. Through his large heart we see into the heart of God and the heart of the Christian message.

Paul founded the church in Corinth about A.D. 50. It was a lively church composed of first-generation Christians but infected with many of the problems associated with a mission. Corinth was the Las

Vegas of the Roman Empire. Some new believers polluted the church with their secular standards in business and sexuality. They argued that all things are permissible in Christ. Others got superspiritual and boasted about their visions, prophecies, words of knowledge and spiritual experiences. In the course of time they wrote Paul asking for advice. Paul wrote 1 Corinthians in about A.D. 55 to address these questions and various problems. Then it seems the Corinthians turned against the founding apostle, a crucial fact to know in order to understand 2 Corinthians. This letter was born in hurt.

Paul paid a second "painful visit" (2 Corinthians 2:1) and wrote a "sorrowful" letter, now lost, from Ephesus (2:4). It is highly likely that Paul then came to Macedonia (2 Corinthians 7:5), modern Greece, where he was reunited with Titus from Corinth and from which he wrote 2 Corinthians, probably while in Philippi.* Later in A.D. 56 Paul visited Corinth again to receive their gifts for the poor Christians in Jerusalem.

As 2 Corinthians was written, Paul had several problems with the Corinthians: he changed his travel plans and did not come when he said he would (2 Corinthians 1:12—2:4); they failed to discipline the person who caused a grievous offense (2:5-11); their contributions for his collection for the Jewish Christians had lapsed (8—9); he accepted financial support from the Macedonians (Thessalonica and Philippi) but not from the Achaians, especially the Corinthians (11:7-11). Paul also conflicted with newly arrived ministers in Corinth who preached a different gospel, probably a return to a form of Judaism (2:14—7:4; 10:1—13:14). Some individual Corinthians criticized Paul because he was a powerful letter writer but a weak speaker who was unimpressive in person.

This relational conflict becomes the medium for revealing the distinctive message of this book: Christ meets us at our point of desperate weakness, *not only before we are saved but after.* Against the false triumphalism of his opponents, Paul proclaims a gospel in which God's power is demonstrated best in human weakness. We have the Christ-treasure in earthen vessels or, as Phillips powerfully paraphrases, "in a common earthenware jar." In a day when authentic Christianity seems less attractive than superspirituality or the "gospel of health, wealth and prosperity,"

Paul's searing honesty offers exactly what the world so deeply hungers for: it tells us how to be real. As we walk through Paul's relationship with the Corinthians step by step, we discover how God in Christ is prepared to meet our deepest relational needs just as we are and where we are.

Suggestions for Individual Study

1. As you begin each study, pray that God will speak to you through his Word.

2. Read the introduction to the study and respond to the personal reflection question or exercise. This is designed to help you focus on God and on the theme of the study.

3. Each study deals with a particular passage—so that you can delve into the author's meaning in that context. Read and reread the passage to be studied. The questions are written using the language of the New International Version, so you may wish to use that version of the Bible. The New Revised Standard Version is also recommended.

4. This is an inductive Bible study, designed to help you discover for yourself what Scripture is saying. The study includes three types of questions. *Observation* questions ask about the basic facts: who, what, when, where and how. *Interpretation* questions delve into the meaning of the passage. *Application* questions help you discover the implications of the text for growing in Christ. These three keys unlock the treasures of Scripture.

Write your answers to the questions in the spaces provided or in a personal journal. Writing can bring clarity and deeper understanding of yourself and of God's Word.

5. It might be good to have a Bible dictionary handy. Use it to look up any unfamiliar words, names or places.

6. Use the prayer suggestion to guide you in thanking God for what you have learned and to pray about the applications that have come to mind.

7. You may want to go on to the suggestion under "Now or Later," or you may want to use that idea for your next study.

Suggestions for Members of a Group Study

1. Come to the study prepared. Follow the suggestions for individual study mentioned above. You will find that careful preparation will greatly enrich your time spent in group discussion.

2. Be willing to participate in the discussion. The leader of your group will not be lecturing. Instead, he or she will be encouraging the members of the group to discuss what they have learned. The leader will be asking the questions that are found in this guide.

3. Stick to the topic being discussed. Your answers should be based on the verses which are the focus of the discussion and not on outside authorities such as commentaries or speakers. These studies focus on a particular passage of Scripture. Only rarely should you refer to other portions of the Bible. This allows for everyone to participate in in-depth study on equal ground.

4. Be sensitive to the other members of the group. Listen attentively when they describe what they have learned. You may be surprised by their insights! Each question assumes a variety of answers. Many questions do not have "right" answers, particularly questions that aim at meaning or application. Instead the questions push us to explore the passage more thoroughly.

When possible, link what you say to the comments of others. Also, be affirming whenever you can. This will encourage some of the more hesitant members of the group to participate.

5. Be careful not to dominate the discussion. We are sometimes so eager to express our thoughts that we leave too little opportunity for others to respond. By all means participate! But allow others to also.

6. Expect God to teach you through the passage being discussed and through the other members of the group. Pray that you will have an enjoyable and profitable time together, but also that as a result of the study you will find ways that you can take action individually and/or as a group.

7. Remember that anything said in the group is considered confidential and should not be discussed outside the group unless specific permission is given to do so.

8. If you are the group leader, you will find additional suggestions at the back of the guide.

---

*This reconstruction follows that proposed by Victor Paul Furnish, *2 Corinthians,* Anchor Bible (New York: Doubleday, 1984), pp. 54–55.

1

Our Comforting God

Life is difficult!" With these three words Scott Peck begins his best-selling book *The Road Less Traveled*. But in 2 Corinthians Paul says this and more. Just where life is difficult, where our relationships are strained, where our competence is questioned, where our health and security are threatened, God makes himself known in powerful comfort.

GROUP DISCUSSION. What has been one of the hardest experiences of your life? Sometimes the most difficult moments turn out to be the best—in terms of growth. How true has this been?

PERSONAL REFLECTION. Recall a time in your life when friends comforted you while you were hard-pressed and despairing. What qualities in their relationship with you enabled them really to comfort you?

In this letter we discover that one of the supreme greatnesses of Christianity is that it does not seek a supernatural escape from the difficulties of life. Instead it offers a supernatural use for them. Troubles become triumphs as God makes himself known in our weakness. *Read 2 Corinthians 1:1-11.*

1. After his customary greeting and "signature," Paul breaks into praise and then recounts his problems. What difficulties did Paul face in the province of Asia (modern Turkey), and why does he praise God?

2. If you were in Paul's situation, what different emotions might you be feeling toward God?

3. Why do you think Paul loves rather than hates God because of all he has suffered?

4. What is the connection between the sufferings of Christ and the comfort of Christ (vv. 5-6)?

5. In what ways have you experienced God's comfort in a difficult situation?

6. Some people respond to suffering by denying it or becoming so self-focused that they are isolated in their pain. What did Paul discover about the meaning of suffering in the Christian life (vv. 8-11)?

7. Why do you think our experience of God's comfort enables us to comfort others who are suffering?

8. How do you think Paul's openness in sharing the realities of his Christian experience affected his relationship with the Corinthians?

How would it have further equipped them as partners in the gospel?

9. Based on what you have learned in these first eleven verses, how can hardships draw you closer to God instead of driving you away from him?

---

10. What must you do to allow your hardest experiences to be transformed into ministry assets?

Think of someone you know who needs comfort. Ask God to comfort that person and to use you in offering comfort, praying that the word of the servant in Isaiah may be yours: "The sovereign LORD has given me an instructed tongue, to know the word that sustains the weary" (Isaiah 50:4).

Now or Later

Of the many solutions given in Scripture of the mystery of pain, this is not the least notable; the sufferer who feels that his sufferings equip him as a missionary of comfort to others will feel that they are well-explained. (Quoted in R. V. G. Tasker, *2 Corinthians*)

Explore the theme of being a fellow sufferer with Christ in other New Testament passages: Romans 8:17; Philippians 3:10; Colossians 1:24; Hebrews 2:9–10; 1 Peter 1:11; 4:13; 5:1.

2

Always Yes
in Christ

Remember Stuart Smalley in the *Saturday Night Live* sketch? He would look into the mirror and chant the following personal mantra: "I'm good enough. I'm smart enough. And, doggone it, people like me." Receiving the unqualified affirmation of a significant other is a fundamental human need.

GROUP DISCUSSION. Recall an experience of being affirmed by another, possibly a parent or a good friend. What made that word or action especially upbuilding for you?

PERSONAL REFLECTION. Pray that you may see yourself as God does and not resist the affirmation of the Holy Spirit.

Often our attempts to affirm each other backfire. Such was Paul's experience with the Corinthians. They regarded his change in travel plans and his tough love as a mixed signal, a yes and no. Paul had already made two visits to Corinth, the first to found the church and another "painful" visit to deal with a serious discipline problem. The latter visit, combined with a difficult letter, resulted in an almost complete breakdown in Paul's relationship with the Corinthians.

Paul had promised to visit them again, twice in fact, first as he made his way to Macedonia and then on his way back. But he changed his plans, delaying his visit and deciding to visit only once. This led his opponents to claim that he was unreliable or fickle. In the process of defending his actions, Paul points the Corinthians to the ultimate ground of our affirmation: the eternal "yes" spoken to us by God in Christ. *Read 2 Corinthians 1:12—2:17.*

1. What problems do the Corinthians have with Paul, and Paul with the Corinthians?

What is Paul's response?

2. Based on 2 Corinthians 1:12-22, what do you think Paul's opponents were saying about his motives and ministry style?

3. What reasons does Paul give for maintaining that his change of itinerary was not a change of mind about the Corinthians (1:12, 17; see also 1:23 and 2:1)?

4. Why do you think Paul directs their attention away from his travel plans to the unqualified yes or "amen" of the gospel (vv. 18-20)?

5. What aspects of Christian experience does Paul point to as evidence of God's yes in Christ (vv. 21-22)?

Which part is most meaningful to you now?

6. In 2:5-11 Paul refers to the discipline of a member of the church, possibly because of a gross sexual sin (see 1 Corinthians 5:1). How does Paul's handling of this problem affirm his love not only for the Corinthians but also for the man who had sinned?

7. Why would Paul's approach to this disciplinary problem likely result in the offender's hearing God's affirmation, his yes, in Jesus?

8. Because Paul had no peace of mind in Troas, he couldn't take full advantage of the "door" the Lord had opened for him (2:12-17). How was he able to speak of his triumph in Christ (v. 14) in the same breath as confessing his weakness?

When has Christ enabled you to triumph in the midst of a personal struggle?

9. What do you think Paul means in saying we are "the smell of death" to some and "the fragrance of life" to others (vv. 15-16)?

How does the thought that Christianity spreads like a fragrance challenge your church or Christian group?

10. What have you learned about the conditions of receiving the affirmation Christ wants to give us?

Praise God for his faithful promises and his yes in Christ.

Now or Later

> It is as if the presence of Christ brought about the strangest of inversions: He wipes out the guilt in the woman who was crushed by it, and arouses guilt in those who felt none. (Paul Tournier)

Look up some of the promises given to God's people, promises that find their yes in your life as you follow Christ:

to to be with us forever (Genesis 28:15, Matthew 28:20)

to accept us on the basis of faith rather than performance (Galatians 2:15-16; 1 Timothy 1:5)

to bless all the nations and to include all peoples in the family of God (Genesis 18:18; 22:18; Galatians 3:8-9; Revelation 7:9)

to give us a place on earth and ultimately to renew all creation (Genesis 15:18; Revelation 21:5; 21—22)

to make a new covenant that will institute a universal every-member ministry (Jeremiah 31:31-34; 1 Peter 2:9-10)

to turn adverstiy into victory (Jeremiah 29:11-14; Romans 8:28)

to deal finally with evil (Revelation 19:11-21)

Make these promises your own and thank God for them.

3

Every-Member Ministry

2 Corinthians 3

Christianity is essentially a lay movement. Every person in Christ is a minister, a priest, a prophet, a prince or princess in the kingdom of God. This every-member ministry takes place not only in the church but in the home, workplace and society—all the places we inhabit from Monday to Saturday.

GROUP DISCUSSION. How do you feel about being told that becoming a Christian means becoming a minister?

PERSONAL REFLECTION. Recall an incident in which you were blessed, helped and touched by God through the care of an ordinary Christian. Thank God for this.

But one would not think that every Christian is a minister while visiting the average church or watching the electronic church on TV. Often the impression we get is that ministry is for the theologically trained, the ordained, the polished and proficient. With the professionalism of ministry in our society, many of us question our ability to minister. Like Paul, we ask, "Who is equal to such a task" (2:16)? In this chapter Paul tells us why all believers are competent for ministry in Christ. *Read 2 Corinthians 3.*

1. In contrast to those who boasted about their letters of recommendation, Paul says the Corinthians are his letter (vv. 1-3). What sort of letter are they?

2. How do you respond to the idea that you may be the only letter from Christ that some people ever read?

3. In 2:16 Paul asked, "Who is equal to such a task?" What answer does he give in 3:4-6?

How could his answer encourage even the newest and humblest member of God's family?

4. According to Paul, how does our ministry under the new covenant contrast with ministry under the old (vv. 3-6; see also Jeremiah 31:31-34)?

5. How does Paul demonstrate that ministry under the new covenant is more glorious than ministry under the old (vv. 7-11)?

6. What does verse 18 reveal about the process and goal of our lives as Christians under the new covenant?

7. What evidence do you see of this glorious transformation (metamorphosis) in your life?

8. Paul speaks of our confidence (v. 4), boldness (v. 12) and freedom (v. 17). Why should each of these characterize our new covenant ministry?

9. What can you do to encourage and equip people in your church to release every member in ministry?

10. How has this passage encouraged you to feel competent to minister as a disciple of Jesus?

Praise God for the transformation he has worked and is still working in you.

Now or Later

Religion can survive for centuries, as a clergyman's or a priest's religion though it survives in a dull state, but when it really thrives it always bursts such bonds. (Elton Trueblood, *Signs of Hope in a Century of Despair*)

Write your own journal entry on 2 Corinthians 3. Here is an example:

This is an amazing philosophy of ministry! It seems to me that it ought to be that Christ is most revealed when we hide ourselves. But that is the Old Covenant with its fading glory, condemnation focus and death–dealing impact. The New Covenant ministry is paradoxically this: as I look at Christ, and as I reveal myself, it is not I who am revealed but Christ. I am like a Kodachrome transparency. If I am looked at, one will see almost no image at all. But if I am held to the light and looked through, a beautiful image begins to appear. This is unself-conscious self-consciousness, the unselfing of the self.

4

This Treasure

Margery Williams wrote a delightful children's story about two nursery animals, a Velveteen Rabbit (after which the book is named) and a Skin Horse, who was very old and very wise. "What is real?" asked the Velveteen Rabbit. The Skin Horse said, "Real isn't how you are made, it is a thing that happens when you are loved for a long, long time. Generally, by the time you are real most of your hair has been loved off, and your eyes drop out and you get loose in the joints and very shabby. But these things don't matter at all, because once you are REAL you can't be ugly except to those who don't understand. Once you are real you can't become unreal again. It lasts for always."*

GROUP DISCUSSION. What does "being real" mean to you?

PERSONAL REFLECTION. Do you feel real in your relationship with Christ? Talk to him about the parts of yourself you feel are shabby. Listen for his loving response.

People marked by weakness, frailty and a kind of living death contain the gospel treasure. Paradoxically, as we shall see, this life situation serves to enhance the message we bring, not detract from it. Once real in Christ, you can't become ugly or unreal again. *Read 2 Corinthians 4:1—5:10.*

---

1. In contrast with the life to come, several images are used by Paul to describe the shabbiness of life now. Note them.

Which do you most identify with?

2. How does Paul's ministry contrast with the practices of evangelists who discredit the gospel (4:2)?

3. What forces does Paul see at work behind those who reject and those who accept his gospel (4:4-6)?

4. In what ways does Paul contrast the glory of the gospel with the weakness of those who preach it (4:7-18)?

5. Why do you think we find it easiest to talk about our strengths and hardest to talk about our weaknesses?

6. We often assume that our weakness will hinder the gospel and detract from it. On the contrary, how does our weakness reveal God's power?

7. How does the experience of "always being given over to death for Jesus' sake" allow the life of Jesus to be revealed in our mortal bodies (4:10-12)?

8. Twice Paul has said we do not lose heart (4:1, 16). On what basis can we be confident that our lives and ministry will not be pointless or fruitless (4:13-18)?

9. In addition to all the troubles of this life (which Paul speaks of as "light and momentary"), there is the inevitability of death and the glory of the life to come (5:1-5). On what basis is Paul so certain of the glory and so confident as he faces the day of judgment (6:8-10)?

10. Why do you think many Christians in the Western world live as though they prefer to be "at home in the body" (5:6), squeezing all they can out of life now?

11. The heavenly-minded have been criticized as being of no earthly use. Malcolm Muggeridge replied that only the heavenly-minded are of earthly use. How does this passage show that he is closer to the truth?

12. Reviewing the entire passage, what do you now understand Paul to mean by saying "we live by faith, not by sight" (5:7)?

How can this perspective help you come to terms with your own weaknesses and mortality?

Praise God for what you have learned about your wonderful future in Christ.

Now or Later

> The glory which is seen, as in a mirror, in Paul's ministry is the glory which shines through suffering. This glory consists in the fact that Paul does not despair in his sufferings, is not abandoned although persecuted, is not destroyed even when struck down. (N. T. Wright, "Reflected Glory: 2 Corinthians 3:18," in *The Glory of Christ in the New Testament*)

In 2 Corinthians Paul affirms that the gift of the empowering presence of the Spirit in the believer is a genuine introduction to the life to come. It is also a guarantee of the full and glorious transfiguration of our persons in Christ. Look up the verses that explain the work of the Spirit in 2 Corinthians (1:22; 3:3, 6, 8, 17, 18; 5:5; 6:6) and in a parallel passage in Romans 8 (8:1, 2, 4, 6, 8, 11, 13-15, 23, 26-27).

*Margery Williams, *The Velveteen Rabbit* (New York: Simon & Schuster, 1975).

5

Ambassadors
for Christ

2 Corinthians 5:11—6:13

Dietrich Bonhoeffer describes the emergence of the superleader under Hitler: "It is essential for the image of the Leader that the group does not see the face of the one who goes before, but sees him only from behind as the figure stepping ahead. His humanity is veiled in his Leader's form."*

GROUP DISCUSSION. Consider your experience of following human leaders. What qualities in these leaders contributed to upbuilding and empowerment? What led to frustration and disillusionment?

PERSONAL REFLECTION. Think of a time when you defended yourself in the context of a strained relationship. To what did you appeal?

In contrast with the superleader Bonhoeffer describes, Paul defends himself by showing his face and declaring himself defended in the gospel but defenseless in himself. In the last study Paul invited us to marvel at the contrast between the glory of the resurrection life of Jesus and these jars of clay. Now he invites us to look into his heart to see how utterly convinced he is about the gospel's message of reconciliation. *Read 2 Corinthians 5:11—6:13.*

---

1. Paul defends his *ministry* and *message* of reconciliation in this passage. What accusations might Paul's opponents have made about his ministry (5:11-13)?

How does Paul answer these accusations?

2. In describing his message, Paul uses the words *reconciliation* and *reconciled* five times (5:18-20). What has Christ done to make reconciliation possible (5:14-21)?

What does it mean to be reconciled to God?

3. What has meant the most to you about your new relationship with God through Christ?

4. Why do you think Paul would tell the Corinthians, who are already Christians, "Be reconciled to God" (5:20)?

5. Why would the Corinthians be more likely to accept Paul as God's messenger if they fully accepted the message he preached?

6. What would it mean for the Corinthians—or us today—to receive the grace of God in vain (6:1)?

7. To what further credentials does Paul point in order to commend himself to the Corinthians (6:3-10)?

Which of these can you identify with? Explain.

8. Reviewing 5:11—6:13 as a whole, what is Paul's strategy as an ambassador for Christ?

9. How might Paul's example help us be more effective ambassadors, especially to people who are "turned off" by Christianity?

Ask God for integrity as an ambassador for Christ.

Now or Later

Review Paul's list of hardships (6:3-10) noting those that are physical, emotional and spiritual. What sense do you make of the paradox of how others see Paul and how he views himself?

In spite of this—or because of it—what gives Paul confidence that he is removing rather than adding barriers before people trying to find their way to God (6:3-4)?

How can you remove barriers in your own life?

> Referring to the words of Charles Wesley's familiar hymn, James Denney says, "It is the voice of God, no less than that of the sinner, which says, 'Thou, O Christ, art all I want; more than all in Thee I find'" (*A Man In Christ*).

---

*Quoted in Ray Anderson, *Minding God's Business* (Grand Rapids, Mich.: Eerdmans, 1986), p. 5.

6

Good Grief

A great theologian once said, "To be a sinner is our distress, but to know it is our hope!"

GROUP DISCUSSION. Why do you think people deny and cover up things that are not right in their lives?

PERSONAL REFLECTION. Recall an experience of deep sorrow, possibly a significant loss, hurt or disappointment. What were some of the good things, if any, that came after the sorrow had passed?

In the last two studies we explored the extraordinary openness demonstrated by the apostle in revealing his own hurts, struggles and weaknesses. His argument for Christian vulnerability is incontestable. We have nothing to lose and everything to gain if we are in Christ and walking into the light. But the Corinthians were equivocating in their handling of an internal scandal. They were tempted to cover it up and not call it sin. In response, Paul patiently and effectively ministered to the Corinthians, urging them not to cover up the problem. The result was what Paul calls godly sorrow, a subject we will explore in this study. *Read 2 Corinthians 6:14—7:16.*

1. What difference does Paul say that our relationship with God should make when we contemplate marriage or relate to brothers and

sisters in the church?

---

2. Second Corinthians 6:14—7:1 is usually understood to apply to marriages between believers and unbelievers. However, what other types of close relationships or partnerships might Paul have in mind?

---

3. What reasons does Paul give for avoiding such unions (6:14-16)?

---

4. How might such relationships lead to disharmony, conflict and compromise?

---

5. Although we may forfeit certain relationships, what positive promises does the Lord give us (6:16—7:1)?

Which of these promises gives you hope when you face hard choices in close relationships?

6. It is often counterproductive to try to persuade someone not to marry a person they deeply love, even if the intended partner is unsuitable. What clues does this passage give us for ministering to someone who is tempted to marry outside the faith?

7. In 2 Corinthians 7:2-16 Paul recalls how comforted he was when he met Titus in Macedonia and heard news of the Corinthians. What makes Paul so "confident," "proud" and "encouraged" (7:4) about the Corinthians?

8. Referring to their response to his "sorrowful letter" (7:8), Paul compares worldly sorrow with godly sorrow (7:9-10). What are the positive indications and constructive results of godly sorrow (7:10-11)?

What makes worldly sorrow so destructive?

---

9. In dealing with a disciplinary matter, such as the marriage of a believer to a nonbeliever (6:14—7:1), what approach would be most likely to lead to worldly sorrow?

---

10. If godly sorrow is so beneficial, why do you think most Christians shrink from the relational work, discipline and tough love that are required to bring it about in others?

---

11. In what areas of your life are you most in need of godly sorrow? What will you do about this?

Ask God for assurance of his great promises and for godly sorrow where you have been living out of harmony with God's will and purpose.

Now or Later

Read other New Testament passages that deal with church discipline (Matthew 18:15-20; 1 Corinthians 5:1—6:11; Galatians 6:1-5). What have you learned about the relational qualities that will bring the best out of these tough situations?

7

The Need to Give

We like to keep our privacy when it comes to talking with other Christians about our finances. The problem of money is compounded by hard-sell media evangelists raising funds for their personal empires. We even try to hide from God; you might say that the fig leaf has slipped from the genitals to the wallet.

GROUP DISCUSSION. Why is it so hard to reveal how much money you have and what you do with it? Where does this reticence come from?

PERSONAL REFLECTION. What positive and negative feelings do you have about people raising money for a Christian cause?

Paul devotes two whole chapters to the grace of giving because both he and the Corinthians have a problem in this area. Paul has been tramping throughout the Gentile churches raising money for the poor Jewish Christians in Jerusalem, many of whom have lost their jobs and homes for the faith. But the Corinthians haven't produced a red cent! That is *their* problem, because they are denying themselves the joy of "this grace of giving" (8:7). Paul's problem is that he has been boasting to the Macedonians (Philippi and Thessalonica) about how much the Corinthians were going to give (9:2-3). As Paul sets out to resolve this problem, he meets not only the Corinthians' need to give but ours as well. *Read 2 Corinthians 8:1—9:15.*

1. What methods does Paul use to encourage the Corinthians to give to the poverty-stricken Christians in Jerusalem?

To what motives does he appeal?

2. In what ways are you challenged in personal stewardship by Paul's passionate appeal?

3. In what ways are the Macedonians excellent examples of generosity (8:1-5)?

Why is Jesus Christ the supreme example of sacrificial giving (8:9)?

4. In both chapters Paul refrains from using the word *money*. Instead he speaks of *sharing* (8:4; 9:13), *service* (8:4, 18; 9:1, 12-13), *offering* (8:19), *grace* (8:6-7) and *gift* (8:12, 20; 9:5). What insights do these words give us into the nature of giving?

5. Paul never raised money for himself, for his own missionary organization or even for Corinth Community Church. What is the primary goal that governs his appeal for gifts (8:10-15)?

What should the principle of equality mean to us as we consider our bond with believers throughout the world?

---

6. What care does Paul take to avoid any suspicion of dishonesty or self-interest as he handles this large gift (8:16-24)?

What would be an equivalent strategy in our own day?

---

7. Some people teach that giving money to the Lord's work results in your getting more money yourself. What does Paul say about the personal benefits of giving (9:6-11)?

---

8. In addition to meeting their material needs, what benefits does our giving produce in others (9:12-14)?

---

9. Paul encourages *cheerful* giving (9:7). The Greek word for "cheerful" is the root of our English *hilarious*. It is the exact opposite of calculated giving under compulsion. According to these two chapters, how could you become a more cheerful giver?

10. How should these chapters guide the planning of your church budget?

Pray for the needs of believers around the world, especially those struggling with persecution and poverty.

Now or Later

> The idea that the service to God should have only to do with a church altar, singing, reading, sacrifice, and the like is without doubt but the worst trick of the devil. How could the devil have led us more effectively astray than by the narrow conception that service to God takes place only in church. . . . The whole world could abound with services to the Lord. (Martin Luther)

Note the rich diversity in the early church of ways of supporting other Christians in the work of God's kingdom: (1) diversity in kinds of support: traveling expenses (Titus 3:12-14), hospitality (Matthew 10:9-10; 3 John 6-8), living expenses (rather than salary for work performed, Romans 16:2; 1 Corinthians 9; 1 Timothy 5:17-18); (2) diversity in ways of receiving and giving support: one church "speeding" you on the way to another, one church supporting you while you are in another church (for example, the Philippians supported Paul in Thessalonica and Corinth), being supported by the church you serve (Paul defended this but made this his exceptional pattern), a ministry team supporting one another (as Silas and Timothy possibly supported Paul in Acts 18:5; women supported the male disciples of Jesus, Luke 8:3); (3) diversity in models: fully supported (Peter, 1 Corinthians 9:5), largely self-supporting (Paul, Barnabas), completely tentmaking (Aquila and Priscilla, Acts 18:2-3).

What practical steps can you and your church take to express support for resident and traveling Christian workers beyond raising salaries for overseas missionaries and providing for your pastor?

8

Spiritual Warfare

2 Corinthians 10

While serving God in the church and world, people encounter subtle resistance and, sometimes, outright opposition. The Christian life is not a victorious life but a victorious battle!

GROUP DISCUSSION. What difficulties have you faced as you have tried to serve God at home, in the church or the workplace? What pressures did you find most overwhelming?

PERSONAL REFLECTION. Personal comparisons are often extremely hurtful. When have you experienced this and how did you respond?

Sometimes when things seem to be getting better we hear news that the situation is worse than we thought. While Paul was writing this letter, he got fresh news that some outside leaders, some so-called super-apostles, had usurped his rightful place. The tone of the letter becomes more assertive and passionate. Now Paul engages in spiritual warfare with principalities, powers and persons who oppose not only Paul but Christ himself. Unlike many of us, Paul wants to *make* peace, not simply *keep* the peace by covering over the problem. We have much to learn from Paul's pastoral strategy. *Read 2 Corinthians 10.*

1. Survey the chapter to see what qualities, according to Paul, characterize truly successful people.

2. What apparent disadvantages did Paul suffer in comparison to his opponents in Corinth? (See especially verses 1 and 9.)

3. Paul says he is not waging war "as the world does" (v. 3). What types of worldly weapons and strategies do you think he has in mind?

In what situations are we tempted to use these tactics today?

4. What is Paul's strategy in this spiritual warfare (vv. 4-6)?

5. Trace, in verses 7 and 10, the arguments of Paul's opponents. Why must Paul "demolish" their arguments and pretensions?

6. What similar arguments and pretensions oppose the knowledge of God today?

7. How can we demolish these strongholds in our churches, neighborhoods and workplaces?

8. Which of your own thoughts need to be "taken captive" (v. 5) to obedience to Christ?

9. Notice the repetition of the word *boast* in verses 7-18. What is wrong with the boasting of Paul's opponents?

10. According to Paul, what is the proper way to determine the success of ministry?

11. How can we boast "in the Lord" (v. 17)?

Ask God to guard your words that your boasting might be only in the Lord.

Now or Later

In many of his letters Paul deals with the complexity of evil. In Ephesians 6:10-18 Paul says that our struggle is not simply against sinful people but also with supernatural powers. The powers—both structures and invisible spiritual beings—were originally good (Colossians 1:15-17) and potentially still are for our benefit: government, law, leaders, authorities and angels. But they have been colonized by Satan, have become resistant and have taken on a life of their own. Even Christian leaders may become instruments of these centers of resistance, as Paul's opponents had in Corinth (see 11:14-15). In Colossians 2:13-15 Paul uses three images to demonstrate Christ's "disarming," "making a public spectacle of" and "triumphing over" the powers. In what ways does Paul's battle with his opponents in Corinth show that in Christ we actually do overcome?

9

Super-Leaders

2 Corinthians 11

In his book *Servant Leadership* Robert K. Greenleaf wrote, "We live in the age of the anti-leader, and our vast educational structure devotes little care to nurturing leaders or to understanding followership."*

Most people in the Western world are double-minded about leadership—fascinated but fearful, wanting strong leadership but guarding themselves from it by protective fences.

GROUP DISCUSSION. What feelings do you get when you hear that a charismatic leader is accumulating a huge following?

PERSONAL REFLECTION. In your own life how have you responded to strong, boastful leadership in church, business or societal organizations? What can you learn about yourself from these experiences?

In this chapter Paul continues to respond to the fresh news he has from Corinth. He not only shows how the super-apostles are not their true leaders but also gives us a basis for identifying real Christian leadership. *Read 2 Corinthians 11.*

---

1. What are Paul's motives for challenging the so-called super-apostles (vv. 1-6)?

2. What does Paul regard as the real hazard of the super-apostles who were winning over the Corinthians?

How does Paul address the root problem in this chapter?

3. How does Paul express his long-term goal of ministry in Corinth (vv. 2-3)?

4. Why do you think betrothal rather than marriage is such a good image of the goal of Christian ministry?

What metaphor or image would describe your own relationship to God at this time?

5. Why do you think Paul's decision to "preach the gospel free of charge" was so important in defending his ministry (vv. 7-12)?

---

6. When would it be right for a Christian leader to be financially supported by his followers?

---

7. What kind of Christian leadership today might fall under the apostle's judgment as false, deceitful and masquerading (v. 13)?

---

8. The Corinthians might not have agreed with Paul's assessment of the super-apostles. What words might they have used to describe their experience of being led by these charismatic giants?

---

9. In contrast, what does Paul boast about as the mark of his own leadership (vv. 16-33)?

Why would his escape from Damascus (vv. 32-33) be such a good example of this?

10. What have you learned from this study about the marks of true Christian leadership?

What have you learned about being a healthy follower?

Ask God for the grace and discernment needed to be both a leader (in some contexts) and a follower (in other situations).

Now or Later

Remarkably, when Paul lists the qualifications of Christian leaders in 1 Timothy 3:1-13 and Titus 1:6-9, he does not mention a single spiritual gift and, of course, no educational accomplishments. Read these lists. In contrast to Paul's standards, what qualities are prized today by Christian people?

How can these scriptural character traits be cultivated?

How can such leadership in the church be encouraged?

---

*Robert K. Greenleaf, *Servant Leadership* (New York: Paulist Press, 1977), p. 4.

10

My Burden
Carries Me

2 Corinthians 12

Few people, if any, delight in their weaknesses and unresolved problems. Nevertheless, our toughest life issues can prove to be a spiritual discipline.

GROUP DISCUSSION. What are the "normal" human responses to chronic illness and personal handicaps?

PERSONAL REFLECTION. What have you learned from the most persistent struggles in your life?

Unintentionally a German philosopher captured the genius of Paul's spirituality with these arresting words: "My burden carries me." Normally we think about the difficulty of carrying our burdens. But in reality our burdens carry us to Christ by convincing us that we are not self-sufficient. They are spiritual assets, not liabilities. "When I am weak, then I am strong" is Paul's final distinction between super-spirituality and the real thing. *Read 2 Corinthians 12.*

1. Paul describes his experience of being caught up to paradise by referring to "a man in Christ" (vv. 1-6). What was Paul's experience like?

2. How do you react when a person shares spiritual experiences that seem completely beyond your reach?

3. Why do you think Paul refrains from boasting about such an exalted experience?

4. Opinions concerning Paul's "thorn in my flesh" (v. 7) range from eye disease (Acts 9:9; Galatians 4:15) to defective speech to his ever-present opponents. While no conclusive answer can be given about the details, what do we know about this bitter reality Paul faced?

How does Paul view Satan's part and God's part in his "thorn"?

5. What was accomplished by Paul's repeated prayer to God for the removal of his thorn?

What do we learn from this about the value of persistent prayer in relation to our handicaps, weaknesses and problems?

6. In contrast to Paul's ecstatic experiences, the simple answer to his prayer (v. 9) is considered to be the summit from which we gain the most complete view of Paul's apostleship. What effect did this answer have on Paul himself?

What help do the Lord's words give us in responding to the health, wealth and success gospel that is widely marketed today?

7. In what ways can you envision God taking something evil or destructive in your life and making it serve a good purpose?

8. To what credentials does Paul point while pleading for his rightful place in the Corinthians' hearts (vv. 11-21)?

9. Earlier Paul mentioned his concern about the Corinthians being led astray by a different gospel (11:1-5). What connection do you see between that false gospel and the other concerns Paul expresses in verses 20-21?

10. Reviewing the whole chapter, what kind of weaknesses or prob-

lems can we legitimately expect God to transform into a means of grace?

What kinds of problems or weaknesses should we not expect God to transform?

Pray that you will be strong especially in your weak places and through this serve Christ powerfully.

Now or Later

> Paul ended, rather than began with "Thy will be done." The peace of God is an end and not a beginning. (P. T. Forsyth, *The Soul of Prayer*)

Money figures largely in Paul's complicated relationship with the Corinthians. Verses 11-18 refer to the very serious charge that while Paul never asked for help from the Corinthians, he had kept for himself the offering raised for the poor in Jerusalem. Possibly the false apostles were charging that Paul was getting support, in an underhanded way, through the cooperation of his associates. Paul mentions five times that he has not been a burden to the Corinthians nor has he exploited them. How does he explain his motives for refusing financial support from them?

Under what circumstances would it be wise today to be a self-supporting Christian worker (a tentmaker)?

11

Examine Yourselves

2 Corinthians 13

Imagine life without a final examination. At first it strikes us as a wonderful vacation, like school without tests and report cards. But without accountability life quickly loses its meaning.

GROUP DISCUSSION. How does the thought of preparing for an exam usually strike you? Explain.

PERSONAL REFLECTION. Recall your most challenging performance review at work or final exam at college. What fears and what hopes did you have?

The whole Bible looks toward the final day with vibrant hope. Those genuinely in Christ have nothing to fear and everything to anticipate. But what of those who are not sure or who, like the Corinthians, might have false confidence about the outcome of the final exam? Paul deals with this matter in his final passionate plea. *Read 2 Corinthians 13.*

1. What can the Corinthians expect from Paul's third visit?

2. How does Paul insist that the Corinthians prepare for his coming?

What would it be like to be one of the Corinthians awaiting Paul's visit?

---

3. What proof can Paul give that Christ is really speaking through him (vv. 3-4)?

---

4. Verse 4 sums up the whole book. Why does the cross represent the heart of what Paul has been saying to the Corinthians?

---

5. In what ways do we shrink from our daily cross and find our power elsewhere?

---

6. Paul asks them to examine themselves not so much in their doctrine as in their experience. How could the Corinthians know experientially that they truly belonged to Christ?

7. In what ways does Paul show that he cares more for *their* passing the test than for *his* seeming to pass the test in the eyes of others (vv. 7-9)?

---

8. How is Paul's attitude one more example of the use of authority to build up rather than to tear down (v. 10)?

---

9. In what specific ways does Paul pray they will be built up (v. 11-14)?

How would these things be encouraging to you?

---

10. If you are unsure of your position in Christ, what can you do about it in light of this chapter?

Pray for courage to take up your cross and follow Christ.

Now or Later

Jesus has many lovers of His kingdom of heaven, but He has few bearers of His cross. . . . He finds many comrades in eating and drinking, but He finds few who will be with him in His abstinence and fasting. (Thomas á Kempis, *The Imitation of Christ*)

Many have misunderstood these words of Jesus: "If anyone would come after me, he must deny himself and take up his cross and follow me. For whoever wants to save his life will lose it, but whoever loses his life for me will find it" (Matthew 16:24–25). Since the cross is something to be "taken up" it is not simply resigned acceptance of the hardships and calamities that come our way. Rather it is a positive agreement with God's saving judgment through the death and resurrection of Jesus and our fellowship with Jesus in his sufferings, identifying with Christ in his victorious meekness (see "Now or Later" in study 1). We do this in everyday life, day by day. How can we be at one time "weak in him" and yet powerfully serve others (v. 4)?

For further study see the optional review of this guide at the end of the leader's notes.

Leader's Notes

MY GRACE IS SUFFICIENT FOR YOU. (2 COR 12:9)

Leading a Bible discussion can be an enjoyable and rewarding experience. But it can also be *scary*—especially if you've never done it before. If this is your feeling, you're in good company. When God asked Moses to lead the Israelites out of Egypt, he replied, "O Lord, please send someone else to do it"! (Ex 4:13). It was the same with Solomon, Jeremiah and Timothy, but God helped these people in spite of their weaknesses, and he will help you as well.

You don't need to be an expert on the Bible or a trained teacher to lead a Bible discussion. The idea behind these inductive studies is that the leader guides group members to discover for themselves what the Bible has to say. This method of learning will allow group members to remember much more of what is said than a lecture would.

These studies are designed to be led easily. As a matter of fact, the flow of questions through the passage from observation to interpretation to application is so natural that you may feel that the studies lead themselves. This study guide is also flexible. You can use it with a variety of groups—student, professional, neighborhood or church groups. Each study takes forty-five to sixty minutes in a group setting.

There are some important facts to know about group dynamics and encouraging discussion. The suggestions listed below should enable you to effectively and enjoyably fulfill your role as leader.

Preparing for the Study

1. Ask God to help you understand and apply the passage in your own life. Unless this happens, you will not be prepared to lead others. Pray too for the various members of the group. Ask God to open your hearts to the message of his Word and motivate you to action.

2. Read the introduction to the entire guide to get an overview of the entire book and the issues which will be explored.

3. As you begin each study, read and reread the assigned Bible passage to familiarize yourself with it.

4. This study guide is based on the New International Version of the Bible. It will help you and the group if you use this translation as the basis for your study and discussion.

5. Carefully work through each question in the study. Spend time in meditation and reflection as you consider how to respond.

6. Write your thoughts and responses in the space provided in the study guide. This will help you to express your understanding of the passage clearly.

7. It might help to have a Bible dictionary handy. Use it to look up any unfamiliar words, names or places. (For additional help on how to study a passage, see chapter five of *How to Lead a LifeGuide Bible Study*, InterVarsity Press.)

8. Consider how you can apply the Scripture to your life. Remember that the group will follow your lead in responding to the studies. They will not go any deeper than you do.

9. Once you have finished your own study of the passage, familiarize yourself with the leader's notes for the study you are leading. These are designed to help you in several ways. First, they tell you the purpose the study guide author had in mind when writing the study. Take time to think through how the study questions work together to accomplish that purpose. Second, the notes provide you with additional background information or suggestions on group dynamics for various questions. This information can be useful when people have difficulty understanding or answering a question. Third, the leader's notes can alert you to potential problems you may encounter during the study.

10. If you wish to remind yourself of anything mentioned in the leader's notes, make a note to yourself below that question in the study.

Leading the Study

1. Begin the study on time. Open with prayer, asking God to help the group to understand and apply the passage.

2. Be sure that everyone in your group has a study guide. Encourage the group to prepare beforehand for each discussion by reading the introduction to the guide and by working through the questions in the study.

3. At the beginning of your first time together, explain that these studies are meant to be discussions, not lectures. Encourage the members of the group to participate. However, do not put pressure on those who may be hesitant to speak during the first few sessions. You may want to suggest the following guidelines to your group.

☐ Stick to the topic being discussed.

☐ Your responses should be based on the verses which are the focus of the discussion and not on outside authorities such as commentaries or speakers.

☐ These studies focus on a particular passage of Scripture. Only rarely should you refer to other portions of the Bible. This allows for everyone to participate in in-depth study on equal ground.

☐ Anything said in the group is considered confidential and will not be discussed outside the group unless specific permission is given to do so.

☐ We will listen attentively to each other and provide time for each person present to talk.

☐ We will pray for each other.

4. Have a group member read the introduction at the beginning of the discussion.

5. Every session begins with a group discussion question. The question or activity is meant to be used before the passage is read. The question introduces the theme of the study and encourages group members to begin to open up. Encourage as many members as possible to participate, and be ready to get the discussion going with your own response.

This section is designed to reveal where our thoughts or feelings need to be transformed by Scripture. That is why it is especially important not to read the passage before the discussion question is asked. The passage will tend to color the honest reactions people would otherwise give because they are, of course, supposed to think the way the Bible does.

You may want to supplement the group discussion question with an icebreaker to help people to get comfortable. See the community section of *Small Group Idea Book* for more ideas.

You also might want to use the personal reflection question with your group. Either allow a time of silence for people to respond individually or discuss it together.

6. Have a group member (or members if the passage is long) read aloud the passage to be studied. Then give people several minutes to read the passage again silently so that they can take it all in.

7. Question 1 will generally be an overview question designed to briefly survey the passage. Encourage the group to look at the whole passage, but try to avoid getting sidetracked by questions or issues that will be addressed later in the study.

8. As you ask the questions, keep in mind that they are designed to be used just as they are written. You may simply read them aloud. Or you may prefer to express them in your own words.

There may be times when it is appropriate to deviate from the study guide. For example, a question may have already been answered. If so, move on to the next question. Or someone may raise an important question not covered in the guide. Take time to discuss it, but try to keep the group from going off on tangents.

9. Avoid answering your own questions. If necessary, repeat or rephrase them until they are clearly understood. Or point out something you read in the leader's notes to clarify the context or meaning. An eager group quickly becomes passive and silent if they think the leader will do most of the talking.

10. Don't be afraid of silence. People may need time to think about the question before formulating their answers.

11. Don't be content with just one answer. Ask, "What do the rest of you think?" or "Anything else?" until several people have given answers to the question.

12. Acknowledge all contributions. Try to be affirming whenever possible. Never reject an answer. If it is clearly off-base, ask, "Which verse led you to that conclusion?" or again, "What do the rest of you think?"

13. Don't expect every answer to be addressed to you, even though this will probably happen at first. As group members become more at ease, they will begin to truly interact with each other. This is one sign of healthy discussion.

14. Don't be afraid of controversy. It can be very stimulating. If you don't resolve an issue completely, don't be frustrated. Move on and keep it in mind for later. A subsequent study may solve the problem.

15. Periodically summarize what the group has said about the passage. This helps to draw together the various ideas mentioned and gives continuity to the study. But don't preach.

16. At the end of the Bible discussion you may want to allow group members a time of quiet to work on an idea under "Now or Later." Then discuss what you experienced. Or you may want to encourage group members to

work on these ideas between meetings. Give an opportunity during the session for people to talk about what they are learning.

17. Conclude your time together with conversational prayer, adapting the prayer suggestion at the end of the study to your group. Ask for God's help in following through on the commitments you've made.

18. End on time.

Many more suggestions and helps are found in *How to Lead a LifeGuide Bible Study.*

Components of Small Groups

A healthy small group should do more than study the Bible. There are four components to consider as you structure your time together.

Nurture. Small groups help us to grow in our knowledge and love of God. Bible study is the key to making this happen and is the foundation of your small group.

Community. Small groups are a great place to develop deep friendships with other Christians. Allow time for informal interaction before and after each study. Plan activities and games that will help you get to know each other. Spend time having fun together—going on a picnic or cooking dinner together.

Worship and prayer. Your study will be enhanced by spending time praising God together in prayer or song. Pray for each other's needs—and keep track of how God is answering prayer in your group. Ask God to help you to apply what you are learning in your study.

Outreach. Reaching out to others can be a practical way of applying what you are learning, and it will keep your group from becoming self-focused. Host a series of evangelistic discussions for your friends or neighbors. Clean up the yard of an elderly friend. Serve at a soup kitchen together, or spend a day working on a Habitat house.

Many more suggestions and helps in each of these areas are found in *Small Group Idea Book.* Information on building a small group can be found in *Small Group Leaders' Handbook* and *The Big Book on Small Groups* (both from Inter-Varsity Press). Reading through one of these books would be worth your time.

Study 1. 2 Corinthians 1:1-11. Our Comforting God.

Purpose: To discover how Christian faith brings hope to the hard places of life.

General note. Paul uses the word *comfort* ten times in this short passage. *Comfort* is a relational word that means to stand beside a person when he or she is going through severe testing. Encourage members of the group to share experiences of being comforted. After others have spoken, you might share that in extreme suffering a comforting friend may serve us best by listening, a powerful hint that God may communicate his comfort to us in silence that invites the pouring out of our hearts. Not everyone in the group will be ready to confess the comfort of God in their distress. But first it is important to observe where Paul found his comfort and what response he made to God.

Question 1. The cryptic reference to hardships in Asia has been widely discussed by commentators. The intensity of the experience and its life-threatening character suggest something more tragic than the temporary riot in Ephesus (Acts 19:23). While a grievous bodily sickness is not excluded, it is more likely, as Furnish suggests (2 *Corinthians*, p. 123), that Paul was imprisoned awaiting execution, during which time he may have written Philippians (see Phil 1:19, 30). Since we do not know the details of the suffering, our focus should be the same as Paul's: what suffering *means*, and what God graciously does with people who feel they are as good as dead.

Questions 2-3. These questions hint at what we know by experience to be true: that suffering may lead either to comfort from God or bitterness against God. The passage reveals that the outcome is largely a result of human choice in the light of God's purpose. The next question explores one further key to triumphant suffering: shared life in the new covenant community.

Questions 3-5. The theme of being a fellow sufferer with Christ is explored frequently in the New Testament. It will be explored in the "Now or Later" section. In contrast to the health and success Christianity widely preached today, this letter underlines that believers will have hard experiences of misunderstanding and rejection like Christ. Further, becoming part of Christ's body they will actually share in Christ's sufferings and, consequently, his victory.

The comfort Paul refers to is not merely inner peace or escape from the problem but, as Paul says in verse 6, "patient endurance." In the course of discussing this question, some will think of sufferings that seemingly have no relationship to Christian ministry; for example, physical handicaps, disease or an accidental misfortune. It will be important to establish that the experience of comfort by God and effective ability to comfort others is not limited to sufferings for the gospel, even though this will be the first application of the passage.

Question 7. This question touches the heartbeat of the letter. Paul and the Corinthians are in Christ *together.* In speaking about "sharing" in our comfort, Paul uses the special Greek word for deep partnership and fellowship: *koinonia.* This word expresses the firm hope (v. 7) that whatever we experience in Christ will benefit *others,* not just ourselves.

Question 8. In many places relational Christianity is "in." But Paul's emphasis in sharing is not a veiled form of personal self-enrichment through self-disclosure. Nor is it a gimmick to rebuild shattered relationships by being vulnerable. What Christ offers is not relational joy, a relational anesthetic or a relational technique, but a hopeful relational suffering. All our problems and comforts benefit *us,* not just me. And the *us* implies unconditional belonging within a new covenant people.

Many pastors, if they had experienced Paul's rejection, would move to another church to find acceptance. But relationships in Christ are neither discardable nor interchangeable. Once bonded with Christ we are then bonded with the family of God. No one is in Christ alone. All ministry is mutual. But this is a far cry from the let-it-all-hang-out religion that passes for relational Christianity today. Make sure you discover how effectively Paul empowered the Corinthians for a relational ministry by revealing the depth of his own relationship with them.

Questions 9-10. These two questions form the primary opportunity to apply the teaching of this section. Encourage each person to move beyond "what this means" to "what this means to me." This can be done verbally or in silent reflection. Since some will have hurts too tender to be shared until trust has been deepened in the group, sharing must not be forced. Pray that some will share their own pilgrimage and so refresh other weary souls with the "tongue of the one who has been taught" by God (Is 50:4). When the sharing of one person is prized, others will become more free to do so.

Study 2. 2 Corinthians 1:12—2:17. Always Yes in Christ.

Purpose: To discover the profoundly positive nature of the gospel and those who communicate it.

Group discussion. The group discussion question will require you to be affirming as well. Encourage people to be *specific* about some affirmation they have received: what was said, how and by whom. What feelings and inner responses did they have to being affirmed?

Question 2. Almost every positive argument by Paul presumes some negative criticism. Reading Paul's letters is often like listening to one end of a telephone conversation. But it is not hard to infer from Paul's arguments what is being said on the other side.

Question 3. "Yes and no" may refer back to the words of Jesus: "Let your 'Yes' be 'Yes,' and your 'No,' 'No'" (Mt 5:37). The mark of a worldly man (v. 17), whose decisions are made according to self-interest, is his saying "yes" and "no" with the same breath, promising to revisit Corinth but then calculating an expedient way to avoid it. Eventually Paul reveals that it was to "spare them" that he delayed his visit, although he never flagged in his love for them or reversed his decision to visit them (2:1).

Question 4. Ralph Martin comments that "Paul has more to defend than his reputation. It was bad enough that his detractors attacked him as vulnerable and shifty. . . . It was worse when they went on to insinuate that his message was just as unreliable and unsure. The purpose of vv. 18-22 is to defend the apostolic ministry which, for Paul, was intimately bound up with the message God had entrusted to him and his co-workers" (*2 Corinthians,* Word Biblical Commentary [Waco, Tex.: Word, 1986], p. 26).

Paul is convinced that Christ is the "Amen" (Rev 3:14), which means "let it be so," the "true" (Rev 3:7). In Christ all the promises of God find their fulfillment (Gal 3:8). Therefore *amen* is especially fitting in the context of public worship (1 Cor 14:16) and in pastoral relationships such as the one between Paul and the Corinthians.

Question 5. The three dimensions of experiencing God's "yes" described in verses 21-22 may require some explanation: (1) *anointing* means receiving an important function in Christ through the Spirit (1 Jn 2:20, 27); (2) *sealing* means certifying ownership and pledging protection by the owner; (3) *guaranteeing* means certifying that we will eventually receive our full inheritance in Christ. These three experiential certainties are reason enough to be confident that Paul, and other servants of Christ who live by such a message, can be trusted.

Question 6. Many modern commentaries support the traditional identification of the unnamed offender and offense with the incest case in 1 Corinthians 5:1. However, an alternative view proposed by Ralph Martin (pp. 164-68) and many ancient commentators avoids many of the difficulties of the traditional view. They propose that the offense was some sort of slander perpetrated, whether by word or deed or both, against Paul. Especially relevant is the contrast of the punishments in view: in 1 Corinthians 5 the offender is to be cut off and left to the destructive powers of Satan, while in 2 Corinthians 2:6-8 the offender is to be forgiven and restored. Ralph Martin explains the situation this way: "Paul has been slandered, probably to his face, by an unnamed individual. A majority of the Corinthian congregation has agreed to some sort of disciplinary action against him, but only after the seriousness and wider meaning of the offense has been brought home by Paul's tearful letter. Confident now of the church's obedience, he writes again about the matter, this time urging that the offending party be forgiven and brought back into the Christian community" (2 *Corinthians*, p. 168). Whichever interpretation is chosen, the important thing is to observe the depth of Paul's love for the Corinthians. They wept because he first wept. Their hearts were touched because his heart had first been touched.

Question 7. Dietrich Bonhoeffer said that church membership without church discipline is cheap grace. If there is no repentance, no forgiveness will be experienced by the offender. The easy "yes" of condoning sin is really a "no." Therefore, tough love requires confrontation.

What Satanic schemes (v. 11) was Paul aware of? In this case Satan would have liked nothing better than to have the offender feel so overwhelmed with sorrow that he felt beyond forgiveness. Therefore, both the apostle's and the community's forgiveness were crucial.

Question 8. Paul was eager to see Titus, because he not only was a personal friend but also Titus would bring news about the Corinthians, whose spiritual state greatly concerned Paul. When he could not find Titus in Troas, Paul was so troubled that he could not continue his ministry there. Yet even when he is too upset to minister, he is part of a triumphal procession (v. 14).

William Barclay helps us understand Paul's reference to a *triumphal procession:*

In Paul's mind there is the picture of a Roman Triumph and of Christ as a universal conqueror. The highest honour which could be given to a victorious Roman general was a Triumph. . . . First, there came the state officials and the senate. Then there came the trumpeters. Then there were carried the spoils taken from the conquered land. . . . Then there came pictures of the conquered land and models of conquered citadels and ships. There followed the white bull for the sacrifice which would be made. Then there walked the wretched captives, the enemy princes, leaders and generals in chains, shortly to be flung into prison and in all probability almost immediately to be executed. . . . Then there came the priests swinging their censers with the sweet–smelling incense burning in them. And then there came the general himself.

. . . After him there rode his family, and finally there came the army wearing all their decorations and shouting *Io triumphe!* their cry of triumph. As the procession moved through the streets, all decorated and garlanded, amid the shouting, cheering crowds, it was a tremendous day, a day which might happen only once in a lifetime. That is the picture that is in Paul's mind. He sees the conquering Christ marching in triumph throughout the world, and himself in that conquering train. (*The Letters to the Corinthians* [Edinburgh: Saint Andrew Press, 1962], pp. 204–6.)

Why was Paul able to triumph in the midst of his struggles in Troas? The obvious yet astonishing answer to this question is the genius of the gospel itself: God's grace is demonstrated in weakness (see 2 Cor 12:7-10).

Question 9. The important thing not to miss is that the *same* odor, the same Christ-bearer, is both a deadly fume and a fragrant perfume. William Barclay suggests one plausible interpretation of this:

We have seen how in that [triumphal] procession there were the priests swinging the incense-filled censers. Now to the general and to the victors the perfume from the censers would be the perfume of joy and triumph and life; but to the wretched captives who walked so short a distance ahead it was the perfume of death, for it stood for the past defeat and their coming execution. So Paul thinks of himself and his fellow apostles preaching the gospel of the triumphant Christ. To those who will accept it, it is the perfume of life, as it was to the victors; to those who refuse it, it is the perfume of death as it was to the vanquished. (*The Letters to the Corinthians,* pp. 204-6)

Study 3. 2 Corinthians 3. Every-Member Ministry.
Purpose: To show how Christ has opened up significant ministry to every one of his followers.

General note. Behind the imagery of a letter written on hearts are crucial Old Testament prophecies fulfilled in Jesus: Jeremiah 31:31-33; Ezekiel 11:19; 36:26. Not only are the Corinthians themselves Paul's letter of recommendation, but their own hearts also bear witness to the fulfillment of prophecy in Jesus—that God has established a new covenant by writing his law not with his finger on stone, as he did with Moses and the Ten Commandments, but by his Spirit on their hearts.

Question 1. Paul does not emphasize that they are a letter from him, but a letter from Christ, thereby indicating that Paul's credentials are not his converts but the effect of the gospel in his converts, their existential experiences of the new covenant. (This is developed by C. K. Barrett, *The Second Epistle to the Corinthians,* 2d ed. [London: Adam & Charles Black, 1973], p. 110.)

Question 3. Victor Furnish notes that while Paul wonders how anyone could presume to take up the responsibilities envisioned in 2:14-16, he asserts "that true apostles are only *adequate* because they have been enabled through an adequacy that comes from God" (*2 Corinthians,* p. 197). This was Paul's confidence (3:4) even though he was rejected (temporarily) by his beloved Corinthians.

Question 4. In comparison to the supreme greatness of the new covenant, Paul points to the problems of the old: engraved in letters on stone (v. 7); associated with an extraordinary leader, Moses (v. 13); with fading glory (vv. 7, 13); resulting in condemnation for inadequate performance (vv. 6, 9). In contrast, the new covenant brings true righteousness (v. 9), motivates the heart (v. 3), brings permanent glory (v. 18), equips all the people of God to minister (vv. 5, 12, 18), while the whole person is being transformed into the likeness of Christ (v. 18). .

It is important to realize that on the Damascus road Paul was not converted from Judaism to Christianity but from his own righteousness by works to a righteousness by faith in Christ. He did not reject his own Jewish people (Rom 9), the practices of Judaism or his own role as a rabbi. Rather than rejecting Judaism as inferior, he explains how Judaism was fulfilled and surpassed in Christ (Phil 3:4-11) who, through death and resurrection, instituted a new covenant (Mt 26:28). A covenant is a binding personal agreement to belong together and is typified by the covenant formula in both Testaments: I am your God; you are my people.

Question 5. The person unfamiliar to the Bible will be at a serious disadvantage. You should read Exodus 34:29-35 ahead of time so that you can introduce this question with a short explanation of the Moses and the veil story.

Paul is here using a "from the lesser to the greater" comparison. Under the old covenant there *was* glory, so much so that Moses had to veil and cover his face. But under the new covenant there is far greater glory.

N. T. Wright interprets verses 7-11 with helpful clarity: "The main contrast in the passage is not that between Paul and Moses, but that between the Christians—even those in Corinth!—and the Israelites, both of Moses' day and of Paul's. Paul can use boldness not because he is different from Moses but because those who belong to the New Covenant are different from those who belong to the Old. . . . Moses had to use the veil because the hearts of the

Israelites (unlike those of the New Covenant people) were hardened" ("Reflected Glory," p. 143).

Question 6. This verse teaches us several things about sanctification, the process by which we become holy. First, the sanctification process is a *transformation*. The Greek word Paul uses here is the one from which we get our English word *metamorphosis*. Just as a caterpillar undergoes a metamorphosis in order to become a butterfly, so every believer is being transformed by God. Second, the Spirit is the agent of transformation. Paul says that all this "comes from the Lord, who is the Spirit." Third, the goal of sanctification is "his [Christ's] likeness." Although we were originally created in God's image (Gen 1:26-27), that image was marred by the Fall. However, that image ("likeness") is now being restored in us by the Spirit.

Finally, sanctification is progressive. It does not happen all at once but rather occurs "with ever-increasing glory." Help the group to draw out these important concepts from verse 18.

As we will discover in chapter 4, the glory spoken of in this verse and throughout the chapter is the glory of Christ precisely because it comes through suffering and difficulties in the Christian life. This true glory is not something visible to the naked eye, like credentials or influential ministry, but is seen with the eye of faith when one looks into the heart of another. So Paul's gentle challenge to the Corinthians to see this glory in their apostle opens up authentic ministry for all others who would reflect God's glory.

Question 8. Paul's concern is that both he and the Corinthians should minister *in the Spirit*, who gives confidence, boldness and freedom of proclamation. Help the group to note the many references to the Spirit in the passage. Because the Spirit writes the law on the heart of every believer, this generosity of ministry is the mark of all ministry among the people of God.

Question 9. Many ordinary church members feel they are powerless to change the unbiblical clergy-laity distinction, the first (clergy) giving ministry and the second (laity) receiving ministry. But there is much that can be done to equip one another through affirmation, person-to-person teaching, and exalting the ministry of ordinary members both in the gathered life of the church on Sunday and in the dispersed life from Monday to Saturday.

Question 10. It is crucial to discover what this passage means to us. Once again, Paul's complicated relationship with the Corinthians becomes the medium of an important communication for believers everywhere today: what makes us competent to minister is not our credentials, not even our freedom from struggles and difficulties, but the work of the Spirit writing the law on our hearts. This qualifies us all to become ministers of the new covenant with the apostle himself.

Study 4. 2 Corinthians 4:1—5:10. This Treasure.

Purpose: To help us celebrate our weakness and mortality as a grace opportunity and a ministry asset.

General note. It appears that Paul's freedom and boldness in ministry under the new covenant was misunderstood by the Corinthians as being pushy. In contrast to the religious hucksters who act craftily and deceitfully, Paul claims his boldness comes not from self-interest but the kind of ministry we have under the new covenant. It is a gift and a grace (4:1), not a skill and an accomplishment.

Question 1. Paul uses several descriptors and word pictures in this passage: jars of clay (4:7), hard-pressed, perplexed, persecuted, struck down (4:8), a dying body (4:10). The transforming perspective of this book—and the gospel itself—is that "our light and momentary troubles are achieving for us an eternal glory that far outweighs them all" (4:17).

Question 2. Paul now uses the veil idea in a new way, not merely to symbolize the concealed glory of the old covenant on Moses' face (3:13) but the veiling of the gospel to unbelievers whose minds are blinded by the god of this age. This makes it especially tempting to use deceptive, manipulative methods in ministry rather than to commend ourselves to the conscience, to preach Christ, to serve and to pray for a miracle of illumination (v. 6).

Question 3. Paul wants us to understand that the blindness of unbelievers to the gospel is not mere personal slowness or obstinate willfulness. They are blinded by Satan. By using the phrase *god of this age* Paul is communicating that this age (this world in all its dimensions) has been infiltrated by an evil spiritual being who wants to colonize all the principalities and powers (Eph 6:12) to woo people away from loving God. It will take a supernatural act to remove the "veil" covering the mind of the unbeliever. But this supernatural act is precisely what happens when Christ is preached (4:5). Using the analogy of God speaking light into darkness (4:6) in God's original creation act (Gen 1:3), Paul says that God creates light again whenever the gospel penetrates the unbeliever's mind. Once again Paul delights in the human impossibility of new covenant ministry. Because we are competent in Christ, "we do not lose heart" (4:1, 16).

Question 4. All commentators agree that Paul's basic message in 2 Corinthians is strength through weakness, but the contrast between strong and weak may be a contrast of a worldview, not merely a contrast between so called "strong" people and "weak" people. Reading the whole letter from this perspective (something you may wish to do) reveals many similar contrasts: the letter kills—the Spirit gives life (3:6); the ministry that condemns—the ministry that brings life (3:9); death—life (4:10); outwardly wasting away—inwardly being renewed (4:16); momentary troubles—eternal glory (4:17); what is seen—what is unseen (4:18); earthly tent—eternal house (5:1); light—darkness (6:14); worldly sorrow—godly sorrow (7:10); weapons of the world—divine power (10:4); boasting in weakness—experiencing Christ's power (12:9). It is not only the contrast between the minister's experience of glory and weakness but the intersection of two ages that Paul has in mind, the new and the old, the new giving a radically different perspective on the weaknesses of the old.

Questions 5-6. Help people explore the implications of God's choosing to invest his power only in gold vessels and super-people. Paul is an excellent example of a "jar of clay" since his weaknesses included nervousness (1 Cor 2:3), an unimpressive appearance (2 Cor 10:10) and physical ailments (2 Cor 12:7). The members of the group may wish to write their own list of personal weaknesses. It is a gospel grace to see each item as an opportunity for an excess of power. Our greatest problem becomes our strength. Much service comes from strength in skills. But deep ministry comes from weaknesses transfigured by the indwelling Christ.

Question 7. This question focuses on the nerve of this study. J. F. Collange believes that Paul is countering the claim of his adversaries that the resurrection power of Christ is disclosed through miraculous phenomena, spiritual gifts, signs and wonders. What is so radical in this passage is Paul's assertion, repeated in verses 10 and 11, that the power of Christ's resurrection life is manifested in our *mortal body* (4:10), our *flesh* (4:11), the words being used interchangeably (Furnish, *2 Corinthians*, pp. 255-57). It is precisely as we suffer for and with Jesus (Rom 8:36; 1 Cor 15:30-31; Phil 1:20; 3:10; Col 1:24), not avoiding the troubles and hardships of living for him, that we will experience the resurrection life of Jesus. Superspirituality demands resurrection life without crucifixion. The glory of the Christian message and messenger is the exact opposite! Members of the group will not have to look far for examples of both counterfeit and real spirituality.

As N. T. Wright so helpfully indicates in the quotation at the end of the study questions, Paul sees weakness as identification with Jesus, acting out the pattern of his life, death and resurrection (Phil 2:6-11), descending into service through death, yet exalted in resurrection. It is not that our suffering brings redemption to ourselves (or others) but that it is a sign of our fellowship with Christ and our certain hope of sharing his resurrection life and power. It will be valuable to review your own life to see what struggles and hardships have come directly from following Christ and are actually fellowship with him.

Question 8. This question addresses the chief hazard in all ministry, whether professional or lay: discouragement. If encouragement depends solely on seeing the results of our ministry, we are walking by sight, not faith. But if our goal is to please God (5:9), whether in this life or the next, we walk by faith and will not be discouraged on the day of judgment (5:10).

Paul would rather please God and be ready for that day, even if he now displeases people, than to please people and displease God. While salvation is not lost because one believer's life is not as pleasing as another's (1 Cor 3:10-15), "the solemnity of this judgment should not be overlooked either. The tribunal of Christ for the Christian is needed to complete God's justice, both in terms of holiness and impartiality. The life of faith does not free the Christian from the life of obedience" (Martin, *2 Corinthians,* p. 114).

Question 11. The wonderful paradox in Christian experience is precisely this new covenant perspective that enables Paul and us to be *real* about the difficulties and problems of life now. Without this heavenly perspective, people tend toward one of two extremes: false messianism (they have to solve all the world's problems in their own lifetime), or despair (the problems turn out to be unresolvable). Not only in dealing with our personal mud pots but also with major problems of social justice, this perspective enables us to work on the real issues without burning out.

Study 5. 2 Corinthians 5:11—6:13. Ambassadors for Christ.

Purpose: To discover that the ultimate ground of our defense before people is the gospel itself, shamelessly shared in terms of the realities of our life.

General note. While in 3:1 Paul hints that one criticism leveled against him was his lack of letters of recommendation, we now find Paul's critics were saying he had no religious proofs, no public displays of ecstasy. Paul assures them of his love motive and his confidence not in signs and wonders but in the power of the preached gospel.

Questions 2-3. Reconciliation implies a broken relationship, in this case between God and humanity. This passage is one of the clearest statements of what it means to become a Christian. Because of sin, people are lost, broken, alienated, homeless, estranged. But through Christ, God lovingly reconciled us to himself (5:14, 18), so that we would no longer live for ourselves but for him (5:15). Verse 21 is one of the most concise statements of the great exchange made by Christ on our behalf—our sin exchanged for Christ's righteousness. Gratitude is therefore the primary motive of ministry. Question 5 gives members of the group an opportunity to share their own experience of reconciliation.

Questions 4-5. 2 Corinthians 5:11-21 is one of the great passages of the Bible that has been robbed of its contextual meaning. Without minimizing the depth and riches of the passage, you should help the group to discover that its first meaning is in the context of Paul's own need to be reconciled with the Corinthians. Far from detracting from the greatness of the passage, this exercise will bring new relevance. The context simply will not allow us to interpret 5:11 as persuading men of the truth of Christianity. Paul is convinced that he is commended and approved by God, but the Corinthians looked on him "from a worldly point of view" (5:16): lacking in visions (12:1), eloquence (10:10), letters of commendation (3:1), Jewish birth (11:22) and personal face to face contact with the incarnate Christ (5:16). While Paul's evangelism was marked by joyful sobriety, he was not without ecstatic experiences (5:13). But even these must have been regarded by Paul's opponents as a weakness. His experiences of speaking in tongues (1 Cor 14:18) and heavenly visions (2 Cor 12:7) may have appeared as madness ("out of our mind," 5:13). Yet all his actions were for the benefit of someone else, whether a rapturous intimacy with God or a sane presentation of the truth of Christ. As Ralph P. Martin puts it, "He has done nothing to push himself forward except to be a minister of the Gospel; rather he is intent on seeking to please God and to serve his fellow men" (*2 Corinthians*, pp. 126-27). But the best defense is an offense. Paul will defend himself by refusing to give a defense and by presenting the gospel through which he and we are defended before God.

Question 6. Summarizing the commentators on 6:1, Ralph Martin says, "It is no foregone conclusion that all will cease to live to themselves and live henceforth for Christ. Paul had brought to the Corinthians the Gospel of reconciliation. In essence their failure to 'practice' their profession constituted a denial of the logical implications of the Gospel. Having learned that Jesus died for them, they had not yet died to themselves. And this failure to die was partially exhibited in their failure to have stood by Paul. This 'frustration of grace' is an example of nongratitude for God's love" (Martin, 2 Corinthians, pp. 165-66). Getting sidetracked in discussion of whether someone can lose their salvation or "fall from grace" may be exciting (or depressing) to some, but it takes us away from both the text and the context.

Question 7. In 5:12 Paul states that he is not commending himself on the basis of his strengths. Indeed, if the Corinthians want to boast about him they should note how God's power has been manifested in his weakness. But now in 6:3-10 Paul says that he *has* commended himself by ministering to the Corinthians (and others) *unconditionally.* There is room for them in his heart no matter what the circumstances, no matter what their response. Further, he holds nothing back of his affection toward them, in spite of their mixed feelings toward him. Once more he pleads, even persuades (5:11), that they will reciprocate the hospitality he has shown them.

Questions 8-9. The remarkable thing about this passage, indeed the whole letter, is the vulnerability of the apostle. "We . . . opened wide our hearts to you" (6:11) sums up the matter. People concerned to present Christ are all too aware of the mixed reputation of churches, Christian leaders and media Christians. What is so often lacking is the barefaced vulnerability of the apostle who lets us look right into, and through, his heart to see Christ. Paul equips the Christians and us to be partners with him in the gospel by taking off the veil. This transparency for which the world hungers is within the reach of every Christian.

Study 6. 2 Corinthians 6:14—7:16. Good Grief.

Purpose: To apply godly sorrow to the obedience issues of our own lives.

Questions 2-4. As Fee and Stuart indicate in *How to Read the Bible for All Its Worth* (p. 62), this reference to *yoke* is rarely used in antiquity to refer to marriage. The context as well does not allow us to focus on marriage *exclusively.* However, since marriage is one relationship where unequal yoking could be disastrous, it will be important for you to gain some background on this issue. Intermarriage between believers and nonbelievers is prohibited not only by this text but a continuous strand of teaching and example in the Old Testament (Deut 7:3; Josh 23:12; Ezra 9:2; Neh 13:25). The major concern is that the believer's undivided loyalty to worshiping God will be polluted. Therefore, Paul quotes (in vv. 16-18) several passages (Ex 6:7; Jer 31:33; Ezek 11:20; Zech 8:8; Is 52:11; 2 Sam 7:8, 14) to reinforce the principle of separation. His primary concern is that God dwells *in* the covenant he has made with his people, and he cannot dwell within those who will not make a covenant with him. Paul *never* counsels anyone in Corinth to separate himself from other believers. Separation from heathendom was necessary for spiritual health, but separation from believers is sinful schism. Unfortunately "come out from them" (v. 17) has been scandalously used by believers who counsel separating from disobedient or compromised Christians, something which Paul himself refused to do in his own relationship with the Corinthians.

Questions 5-6. The Old Testament quotations here from Leviticus 26:12; Jeremiah 32:38; Ezekiel 37:27; Isaiah 52:11; Ezekiel 20:34, 41; 2 Samuel 7:8, 14 are rich in *covenant* language. The Bible's main way of describing God's relationship with his people is not a service contract (I want you to do my work on earth in exchange for salvation) but a covenant of belonging (symbolized by the formula "I will be your God, and you will be my people"). The essence of this is belonging, the greatest treasure believers have under the new covenant. While the covenant itself is unconditional (God will not divorce us), the blessings of the covenant are conditional on obedience to the obligations of living as a covenant people. We can forfeit the blessings or, by living the lifestyle of the covenant people, enjoy the blessings of belonging. But the covenant remains in either case.

Question 8. So few people have experienced "good grief" that Paul's phrase needs some interpretation. *Godly sorrow* is a phrase also found in Romans 8:22 and suggests a "grief that leads individuals to view their conduct as God does" (Martin, *2 Corinthians,* p. 230). Paul's purpose in ministering to the Corinthians was not to inspire the regret of self-condemnation and self-hatred, but rather the sorrow that motivates repentance. Contrary to common thought, repentance is not merely remorse over one's wrong, but loving God and his kingdom so much that we gladly turn from sin and, in penitence, lay hold of the gift of forgiveness. It is turning from darkness to light, from self to God, not the other way around. Consider the contrast of the self-destructive remorse of Judas (Mt 27:1-10) and the life-giving call to repentance in the gospel of Jesus (Acts 2:38-47). To condemn sin without proclaiming grace is not only unbiblical, it is dangerous, potentially leaving someone to wallow in his own defeat. This is what Paul means by *worldly sorrow.*

Study 7. 2 Corinthians 8—9. The Need to Give.

Purpose: To discover and apply Paul's great principle of stewardship.

Group discussion. Don't be surprised if people in the group recount horror stories of dishonest Christians or scandalous fund-raising programs. The main point of this question is to establish that it is hard for us to come to this text without negative bias.

General note. Chapters 8-9 must be understood in the context of Paul's collection for the poor Christians in Jerusalem. When Paul was first converted and commissioned to ministry, he checked out his gospel with those who were apostles before him in Jerusalem. They approved of him and required nothing further except that in his Gentile mission he should remember the poor (Gal 2:10), specifically the impoverished Jewish Christians around Jerusalem who had been excommunicated from the synagogue and had lost their jobs and homes.

Paul took this request as a major challenge to build a bridge of mutual ministry between Jews and Gentiles. He argued that if the Jews had contributed to the Gentiles the riches of their spiritual inheritance, the Gentiles, who were comparatively more wealthy, should contribute to the Jews their material inheritance.

While Paul encouraged the support of Christian workers (1 Cor 9:7-14), the primary thrust of all his teaching on stewardship was this love gift from the Gentiles to the Jews. It seems from Acts 20:16 and 21:1-16 that Paul was determined to present this gift personally in Jerusalem at the Feast of Pentecost, perhaps to symbolize that the full measure of blessing of Christ (Rom 15:29) can be experienced only when Jews and Gentiles, and other humanly estranged groups of people, are united in Christ.

Having asked the Corinthians to participate in the collection (1 Cor 16:1-4), having boasted to other churches about what the Corinthians intended to give (2 Cor 8:8; 9:1-3), and having received an extraordinary gift from the Macedonians, who gave generously out of their extreme poverty (2 Cor 8:1-4) and pleaded for the privilege of giving, Paul is now embarrassed that the Corinthians have produced nothing. But it is more than personal embarrassment that motivates Paul to write these two chapters. He is concerned that they are missing the grace of giving.

Question 1. You might remind the group that Paul had none of the benefits of modern communication technology to bring the needs of developing countries to more advanced countries. Also, the emotional distance from Corinth to Jerusalem was many times greater than from a first-world church to a third world church. Yet without pictures and recorded sounds Paul was able to vividly connect the givers and receivers. Old Testament tithes were like taxes paid to the temple; they were not discretionary gifts (for an exception, see Gen 14:20). See the note on question 9. In contrast, Paul encouraged inwardly motivated freedom and generosity that stemmed from gratitude and love (8:9; 9:15). Pastorally, however, Paul does lean on the Corinthians to keep commitments they have made and not to shame him.

Question 5. Later, while writing to the Romans from Corinth, Paul clarified that equality means mutuality, a two-way giving. He said, "For if the Gentiles have shared in the Jews' spiritual blessings, they owe it to the Jews [specifically Jewish believers] to share with them their material blessings" (Rom 15:27).

While Paul uses the word *equality* (8:13-14), he might have chosen to speak of *justice*. He believed it would be wrong for brothers and sisters in Judea to be in grinding poverty while members of the same family in Corinth were living in comparative affluence. While evangelism must always be the center of the church's mission, the circumference is social justice. The church is to become a working model of the justice God wants to bring into the whole earth through Jesus.

You might also point out that Paul's first concern was not toward the haves and have-nots in the world, but toward rich and poor Christians in the church.

Question 6. While in other sections Paul declares he does not care what people think of him, in this matter he takes pains to do what is right "not only in the eyes of the Lord, but also in the eyes of men" (8:20). Direct the discussion toward the way Paul sought to be free of such criticism and why.

Question 7. Direct people to a careful study of the words Paul uses to speak about the personal benefits of giving. Reaping generously (9:6), making grace abound in every good work (9:8), increase your store of seed, enlarge the harvest of your righteousness (9:10), made rich in every way (9:11) all suggest something like having an unlimited grace account with God. Gratitude is the primary motivation for giving (9:15) and life-enrichment is the primary personal benefit.

Question 8. These verses reveal some of the unintended spin-offs of giving:

thanksgiving to God (9:12), recognition of our integrity in evangelism (9:13), and the prayers of those who have received these gifts (9:14). It is challenging to apply these principles to first- and third-world churches today. As we in the first world share our theological and material resources with churches in developing countries, we receive their mature ministry in the Spirit and extraordinary passion for evangelism. Unfortunately, overseas mission today is still largely a one-way street and lacks biblical mutuality.

Question 9. Undoubtedly someone will raise the question of tithing (one-tenth) as the Christian standard of stewardship, or at least an inspired guideline. Significantly the Old Testament tithe accomplished four things that are implicit in New Testament giving: it (1) celebrated the goodness of God (Deut 14:26), (2) acknowledged God's ownership of everything, (3) maintained places of worship (Num 18:21; Deut 14:27) and (4) cared for the poor (Deut 14:28-29). Even in the Old Testament tithing was only part of Israel's stewardship that included care of the land and sharing with the needy. The New Testament only once mentions tithing (Mt 23:23)—in the context of Jesus' calling the Pharisees to something more important. The New Testament principle is not one-tenth but "hilarious giving" (2 Cor 9:7), that is, cheerful and uncalculating. Since everything belongs to God, we should generously disperse what we can to help others. But the use of "should" destroys the very idea of Christian giving; it comes not from law, principle or obligation but from the spontaneous overflow of gratitude for Christ's blessing on our lives (2 Cor 8:9). As Thomas Aquinas so beautifully explained, this holistic stewardship is much more than handouts. He listed the seven corporal alms deeds—visit, quench, feed, ransom, clothe, harbor and bury (the dead)—and linked them with seven spiritual alms—instruct, counsel, reprove, console, pardon, forbear and pray (*Summa* 32.2.1).

Under the new covenant the inspired standard is hilarity and the refusal to calculate—though not the refusal to plan. According to these chapters, our view of God is measured by our willingness to participate in the grace of giving. A small god inspires pinched purses. Paul's concern, and God's, is not the amount (8:12) but the heart attitude. This makes God the ultimate giver (8:9) and the ultimate receiver (8:12).

Study 8. 2 Corinthians 10. Spiritual Warfare.

Purpose: To learn how to engage in spiritual warfare.

General note. Until now Paul's problems in Corinth were *internal;* but the new factor is the presence of high-powered, self-appointed apostles who came in from the outside and were undermining Paul.

Question 2. The identity and details of the "false apostles" in 2 Corinthians has occupied scholars for decades. We know little about their doctrines but much about their personal deportment and relationships, matters of equal importance to Paul. Unlike Paul, who boasted of his weakness (11:30; 12:5) they boasted of their power and extraordinary experiences (12:1). We may reasonably assume that they boasted about better letters of recommendation (3:1), better speaking skills (10:10), a better Jewish background (11:22) and a more direct relationship to Christ (11:23). Undoubtedly they had already scored some successes in winning the Corinthians over to their leadership and their version of the gospel, especially as they went about comparing themselves favorably with Paul (Furnish, *2 Corinthians*, pp. 48-54).

By referring to two character traits of Christ, meekness and gentleness (v. 1; see Mt 11:29), Paul separates himself from his enemies who may have regarded him as self-abasing or groveling, but in a devious way. In contrast, they were strong and self-assertive (10:10). By establishing his self-image on the model of the incarnate Jesus, Paul shows that meekness is not weakness. Because he had received a mandate from the risen Lord, Paul could insist on obedience to the gospel without claiming to be either inferior or superior.

Question 4. Paul's image of pulling down fortresses is probably an allusion to Proverbs 21:22: "A wise man scales the cities and brings down the stronghold in which the ungodly trust." Commenting on this, Ralph Martin suggests that in verse 5 Paul may be changing the metaphor from a fortress of worldly wisdom needing storming, to a "wall of rivalry between himself and his Corinthian converts. His job is to tear it down, since for him this alienation is a sign that the Corinthians are blocking their access to the divine truth of the gospel" (*2 Corinthians*, p. 306). In any event, false belief and unbelief cannot be attacked without dealing with the pretensions of those who would wean others away from apostolic truth.

Question 5. Apparently the self-appointed apostles were denying Paul's apostleship, denying his relationship with Christ (10:7; 11:5; 13:3), capitalizing on Paul's gentleness in dealing with Corinth as though he were weak and lacking in charismatic presence (10:10). Paul's work with his hands was considered as a form of worldliness, an unnecessary humiliation (11:7) and inappropriate for an apostle.

Questions 6-8. You may need to remind people of their answers to questions

4 and 5, where we explored the strongholds that needed to be torn down in Corinth. The twin errors of false inferiority (the cloak of pride turned inside out) and superiority can be avoided by realizing we have no authority in ourselves but, like Paul, only in Christ. It will not be hard to find unworthy examples of people who do spiritual warfare "as the world does" (v. 3). But help the group explore how to use weapons with divine power (v. 4) against the strongholds they encounter.

Now or Later. Historically the church has engaged the powers in a variety of ways: prayer, exorcism, suffering powerlessness (nonviolent), creative participation in the structures of society, and sometimes, when all else has failed, civil disobedience. In Corinth Paul used Spirit-empowered argumentation and personal meekness, a wonderful combination found also in the ministry of Jesus. Prayer is our primary way of putting on the defensive armor and offensive weapons of Christ (Eph 6:13-18).

Study 9. 2 Corinthians 11. Super-Leaders.

Purpose: To learn how to identify and follow true Christian leaders.

General note. Chapter 11 continues Paul's response to fresh news from Corinth. You may want to begin by reviewing some of the important lessons of chapter 10. In that chapter he spoke of his confrontations as demolishing strongholds. But now, in chapter 11, Paul reveals the spiritual reason for his passion: he has betrothed the Corinthians to Jesus Christ, and he does not want them to miss their own wedding day!

Question 3-4. Paul's self-description as a groomsman is reminiscent of John the Baptist (Jn 3:29). In the Old Testament, Israel was the bride of the Lord (Is 54:5; Hos 2:19), and the rabbis compared Moses to a friend of the groom, facilitating the ultimate union. In the New Testament the church is the heavenly bride (Rev 19:7; 21:2), awaiting the great day. But unlike modern engagement, ancient betrothal was no mere statement of intention. Betrothal was presexual marriage and could only be severed by divorce (Mt 1:19). All genuine ministry then is premarital training! This heavenly orientation is one of the most lacking dimensions in Western Christianity.

Questions 5-6. In 1 Corinthians 9:3-18 Paul defended the right of an apostle to be supported by those to whom he preached (see Deut 18:1; Mt 10:10). Yet he refused to use that right so that the gospel would not be hindered. When Paul was in Corinth, he accepted assistance from elsewhere (2 Cor 11:8-9), but turned it down from the Corinthians. The super-apostles, in contrast, not only demanded support (11:20) but also slandered Paul by inferring that he did not accept the Corinthians' gifts because he did not love them (11:11).

Several principles about financial support can be distilled from Paul's teaching and example: (1) a congregation has a duty to support its workers; (2) it is questionable whether one should ever raise one's own support where it is not freely offered (perhaps this is what the super-apostles were doing [11:20]); (3) the advancement of the gospel must be the reason for receiving support when it is offered; and (4) since it may be that Paul would accept support from a congregation *after* he had moved to plant a church elsewhere (1 Thess 2:9), though Paul had no plans of ever receiving support from the Corinthians (11:9; 12:13), being supported by one community to serve another is one commendable option. There is much here to correct the religious entrepreneurialism of Western Christianity.

Question 8. Verse 20 is a succinct summary of five things that false leaders will do to their followers: (1) instead of giving freedom they take away freedom; (2) they exploit their followers; (3) they take advantage of their followers; (4) they promote themselves; and (5) they put others down ("slap you in the face") while they build themselves up. People under the aura of a charismatic and controlling leader are likely unaware of the terrible price they are paying as followers.

Question 9. Once again, the central theme of the book—strength through weakness—surfaces. Paul's boasting in his sufferings is not a disguised form of self-pity or a martyr complex, but a solemn affirmation that he is one with Jesus. Therefore strength comes through weakness and life through death.

Study 10. 2 Corinthians 12. My Burden Carries Me.

Purpose: To discover how our weaknesses can become the means of experiencing God's grace and power.

General note. In chapter 12 Paul continues his "fool's speech" in which he boasts as the world does (11:18), having turned his boasting inside out by boasting of the things which show his weakness (11:30). In chapter 11 Paul ·established the principle of strength through weakness. In chapter 12 he explains how the principle was born in the crucible of his own experience.

Question 2. A careful distinction must be kept throughout this study. On the one hand, firsthand spiritual experiences—even ecstatic "heavenly" ones— are, through the grace of the new covenant, a potential for every person in Christ, not merely an elite group (Joel 2:28; Acts 2:17). On the other hand,

Paul is emphatic that his authority is not derived from his experiences of Christ but from the Christ of his experiences. Though Paul has seen the risen Christ in a truly apostolic experience (1 Cor 9:1; 15:8), he asks to be judged by his faithful service in the gospel (12:6).

Someone has said that the best way to have spiritual experiences is not to seek them but rather to seek the Lord. He will give us the experiences we need. What we need is an experience of Christ that leaves us adoring Christ, not our experience. For Paul, as this chapter illustrates, this was the experience of power in weakness—not exactly what he wanted but exactly what he needed.

Question 3. If needed, you might follow up this question by asking, On what basis does Paul believe he should be evaluated by the Corinthians (v. 6)?

Questions 4-5. For a complete discussion of Paul's thorn see Ralph P. Martin, *2 Corinthians*, Word Biblical Commentary (Waco, Tex.: Word, 1986), pp. 411-16.

It is important to observe that Paul's thorn was evil, not neutral; a messenger of Satan sent to buffet him. Yet the thorn served a good purpose. *There was given* (v. 7) hints at God's overarching reason for allowing this thorn and refusing to remove it: first, the thorn kept Paul from becoming conceited (v. 7); second, it caused Paul to rely on and even delight in God's power displayed in weakness (vv. 9-10).

Question 6. Those even vaguely familiar with the Lord's words to Paul may pass over their dynamic impact. On the emotional level many Christians (and many who are considering becoming Christians) believe that Christ delivers from trouble and hardship. In contrast, Paul emphasizes that God's power is often given *in the midst of our weakness*. Much that passes for Christianity today is baptized paganism. The real thing is God's power displayed in the midst of weakness.

Question 8. Signs, wonders and miracles were *part* of Paul's apostolic credentials, but not the whole. In this epistle especially, Paul minimizes the spectacular and maximizes the credential that is within reach of all Christians: extravagant self-giving (v. 15).

Now or Later. In all their dealings with the Corinthians, Paul and his associates were able to prove their complete integrity. In contrast, the false apostles then and now have too much to lose to leave their financial records open to public scrutiny (see the "Now or Later" notes in study 7).

Study 11. 2 Corinthians 13. Examine Yourselves.

Purpose: To establish and put into practice a biblical basis for self-examination and fruitful service.

Question 1. It seems that chapter 13 takes us back to travel plans again, that complicated issue raised in 1:15-21. But now, with fresh news from Corinth, Paul is less apologetic and more confrontational. He will not "spare" them such a visit, if they need it, because they have challenged his apostolic authority and therefore have jeopardized their faith. Already he has visited them twice, first to found the church, and second to deal painfully with their disciplinary problems. That second painful visit seems to have been unsuccessful and thus was cut short. Since the wrongdoers were not yet repentant (12:21), and his adversaries were capitalizing on the problem, Paul says he will come again to begin judgment, if necessary, using the Deuteronomy 19:15 principle of two or three witnesses for every charge. While they think he lacks proof that he is Christ's apostle in ecstatic speech, spiritual gifts and miraculous deeds (12:12), they will have ample proof that he speaks for Christ when he deals decisively with impenitent sinners!

Question 3. Paul has conceded to the church the right to examine his work but, as Ralph Martin proposes:

> the nub of the debate is that the criteria chosen by the Corinthians to evaluate his work are wrong (10:12; 11:12, 17; 12:11-18). They had been swayed by the opponents of Paul and thus used their supposed miraculous gifts and powerful speech as standards to judge that Paul was 'inferior.' But this conclusion drawn by the Corinthians was wrong, in Paul's estimation. The only test of the validity of any ministry is whether it conveys the word of Christ to his people. In this light, had not Paul brought the word to the Corinthians (1 Cor 2:4) and thus been part of the reason for their conversion (1 Cor 4:15; 15:11; 2 Cor 3:1-3)? (*2 Corinthians,* p. 473.)

Question 4. Behind Paul's discussion is the Corinthian's triumphalism, their boast that they are strong in Christ (1 Cor 4:10). Furnish comments helpfully on the subtle but crucial point of difference Paul has with them. "In claiming this, they think of themselves as possessing Christ's power in such a way as to reign with him (1 Cor 4:8). For Paul, however, believers do not *rule with* Christ's power (the point of the irony in 1 Cor 4:8-13) but are to be *ruled by it* (cf. 2 Cor 5:14); and so he writes here of Christ being powerful *toward* or *among* (not "in") them" (*2 Corinthians,* p. 576. Emphasis mine).

Paul and the Corinthians understand power very differently. For the

Corinthians, power is energy in actions, spectacular spiritual gifts and forceful personalities. For Paul, the shape of power is always cruciform. Jesus was not weak but chose to be weak and vulnerable on the cross in order that God's mighty power would be effectual through resurrection and ascension. Similarly Christ's true apostle will not only appear weak, much to the pleasure of his opponents; he *is* weak. But because he is weak, he lives by God's power. In the same way true believers in Corinth will join Paul in identifying with the crucified Jesus and discovering not that they are powerful in Christ, but that Christ is powerful in them.

Question 6. A serious mistake made by many well-meaning personal evangelists is to offer assurance by convincing and persuading. Paul does the exact opposite. He invites the Corinthian disciples to see if they have the experiential assurance that God gives. Unlike the spurious assurance offered by fellow human beings, often appealing to reason or confidence that "you have done all that God asks," genuine assurance is the gospel experience: living in Christ by God's power in our weakness (v. 4).

Question 7. In exploring this question, make sure you do not miss Paul's absolute confidence that the truth of Christ is indestructible (v. 8). Here is the secret of Paul's strange apology for himself, which is the reverse of normal self-defense. Paul can afford to become a fool because, in the end, Christ's power can be displayed even through his demise. Thus the irony of being considered a fool for Christ is that the fool speaks the ultimate wisdom and his "wise" critics turn out to be tragic fools.

Question 10. Review the note on question 6. While this passage does not lead to "three easy steps to make sure you are a Christian," it does provide the framework for real faith. Being a Christian is having Christ in us ("Christ Jesus is in you," v. 5), a relationship of grace, not a reward for performance. The miracle of this relationship is founded on the cross and resurrection (v. 4), expressed in chapter 5 as a double substitution (5:21). The experience of this relationship is one of God's power in weakness: God with us.

Now or Later. You may want to take another session to complete the review study below. These study questions form a review of the entire book, one question for each study. While many themes are explored in 2 Corinthians, the truth that is strained through Paul's large heart suggests the theme for this final study: what is a Christian like on the *inside*. Do not linger at length on any one question, but try to review the book as a whole, noting and encouraging personal sharing and personal benefits gained. You may wish to conclude by reading a few representative verses, thanking God for what he has revealed: 1:3, 20; 3:6; 4:7; 5:1-5; 7:2-4; 8:8-9; 10:3-6; 11:2-3; 12:8-10; 13:4, 11-14.

Final Review. 2 Corinthians 1—13. Reviewing This Unfinished Motion Picture.

Purpose: To establish the long-term benefits of having studied 2 Corinthians.

Finding out what a person is really like on the inside can be a disarming experience, sometimes profoundly upsetting.

GROUP DISCUSSION. What do you find hardest to hear from a highly respected person when he (or she) reveals his inmost thoughts?

PERSONAL REFLECTION. Speak to God about your inmost thoughts and deepest struggles. When would it be valuable to share these not only with God but others?

The introduction noted that 2 Corinthians gives us the inside view of a first-century Christian—the apostle Paul. But this is no snapshot, no still picture, but rather a motion picture of a person in process. Second Corinthians was written at more than one sitting, as Paul responded to fresh pressures and problems. We see him (and the Corinthians) at his worst, with his feelings bent out of shape, not frozen into a verbal portrait but rather expressed dynamically, sometimes hanging out awkwardly. This exquisite transparency is the genius of the apostle. It is also the genius of this lovely letter and of the faith Paul longs for his dear Corinthians—and us—to wholeheartedly embrace. A short review will firm up its abiding value to us in exploring what the Christian life is like *on the inside.*

1. Now that you have completed studying the letter, what new insights do you have into the comfort of God experienced by the Christian (1:1-11)?

2. As followers of Jesus, how can we hear God's affirmation, his "yes" in the realities of our daily life (1:12—2:17)?

3. How have you been encouraged to become more bold through discovering that you are a letter from Christ, a person who reflects God's glory to those around you (3:1-18)?

4. How has knowing that we have "this treasure in jars of clay" affected your view of ministry (4:1—5:10)?

5. What kind of ambassador for Christ will commend the Christian faith to the world (5:11—6:13)?

6. What have you learned about experiencing godly sorrow rather than worldly sorrow (6:14—7:16)?

7. Paul says that God loves a hilarious giver (9:7). What have you learned about the sources of Christian generosity (8:1—9:15)?

8. Christians can be tough and tender at the same time. How do you think it is possible to tear down strongholds and to build people up at the same time (10:1-18)?

9. What stereotypes or caricatures of spiritual leaders have been challenged by this letter (11:1-33)?

10. Paul's great watchword is, "When I am weak, then I am strong" (12:10). When have you seen God's power displayed in the midst of your weaknesses (12:1-21)?

11. According to Paul, what is God looking for in the life of a follower of Jesus (13:1-14)?

12. How has this letter added to your understanding of what it means to live by faith?

Thank God for the discoveries you have made through this study.

Now or Later

Using a Bible dictionary, handbook or concordance, research one of the following key words in this book: comfort (1:4), Spirit (1:22), ministry (3:6), glory (3:11; 4:17), judgment (5:10), love (5:14), reconciliation (5:18), righteousness (6:7), holiness (7:1), repentance (7:10), saints (8:4), equality (8:14), grace (9:8; 12:9), meekness (10:1), Satan (11:14), signs (12:12), witnesses (13:1), authority (13:10). Turn your discoveries into a prayer to be a person through whom Christ is revealed to others and the world.

R. Paul Stevens, husband and father of three, grandfather of eight, teaches applied and spiritual theology at Regent College in Vancouver, British Columbia, and is the author of many books, including The Complete Book of Everyday Christianity, The Other Six Days *and the LifeGuide® Bible Studies,* Revelation, Job, End Times *and* 1 Corinthians.